HAPPY READING
FROM YOUR FRIENDS
AT
THUNDER HILL ELEMENTARY SCHOOL!
DECEMBER 2, 2009

Classic
Nursery
Rhymes

Classic
Nursery
Rhymes

GRAMERCY BOOKS

NEW YORK

Published by Gramercy Books, an imprint of
Random House Value Publishing, a division of Random House, Inc.,
New York, by arrangement with Arcturus Publishing Limited.

Gramercy is a registered trademark and the colophon is a
trademark of Random House, Inc.

Random House
New York • Toronto • London • Sydney • Auckland
www.randomhouse.com

Cover design: Steve Flight
Art director: Peter Ridley
Design: Maki Ryan
Illustration: Ulkutay & Co Ltd
Compiler: Paige Weber
Editor: Rebecca Gerlings

Printed and bound in China

A catalog record for this title is available from the
Library of Congress.

ISBN-13: 978-0-517-22729-9
ISBN-10: 0-517-22729-0

10 9 8 7 6 5 4 3 2 1

CONTENTS

CONTENTS (continued)

Jack and Jill

Jack and Jill went up the hill,
To fetch a pail of water.
Jack fell down and broke his crown,
And Jill came tumbling after.

Then up Jack got, and home did trot,
As fast as he could caper,
Where his mother covered his head,
With vinegar and brown paper.

Old King Cole

Old King Cole was a merry old soul,
And a merry old soul was he.
He called for his pipe, and he called for his bowl,
And he called for his fiddlers three.
Every fiddler, he had a fine fiddle,

And a very fine fiddle had he.
Twee-tweedle-dee, tweedle-dee, went the fiddlers,
Tweedle-dum-dee, dum-dee-deedle-dee!
Oh, there's none so rare as can compare,
With King Cole and his fiddlers three!

Pat-a-Cake

Pat-a-cake, pat-a-cake, baker's man,
Bake me a cake as fast as you can.
Roll it and pat it and mark it with B,
And put it in the oven for baby and me.

Georgie Porgie

Georgie Porgie, pudding and pie,
Kissed the girls and made them cry.
When all the boys came out to play,
Georgie Porgie ran away.

Hey, Diddle, Diddle

Hey, diddle, diddle,
The cat and the fiddle,
The cow jumped over the moon.

The little dog laughed,
To see such a sport,
And the dish ran away with the spoon.

15

Eency, Weency Spider

Eency, weency spider,
Went up the water spout.
Down came the rain,
And washed the spider out.

16

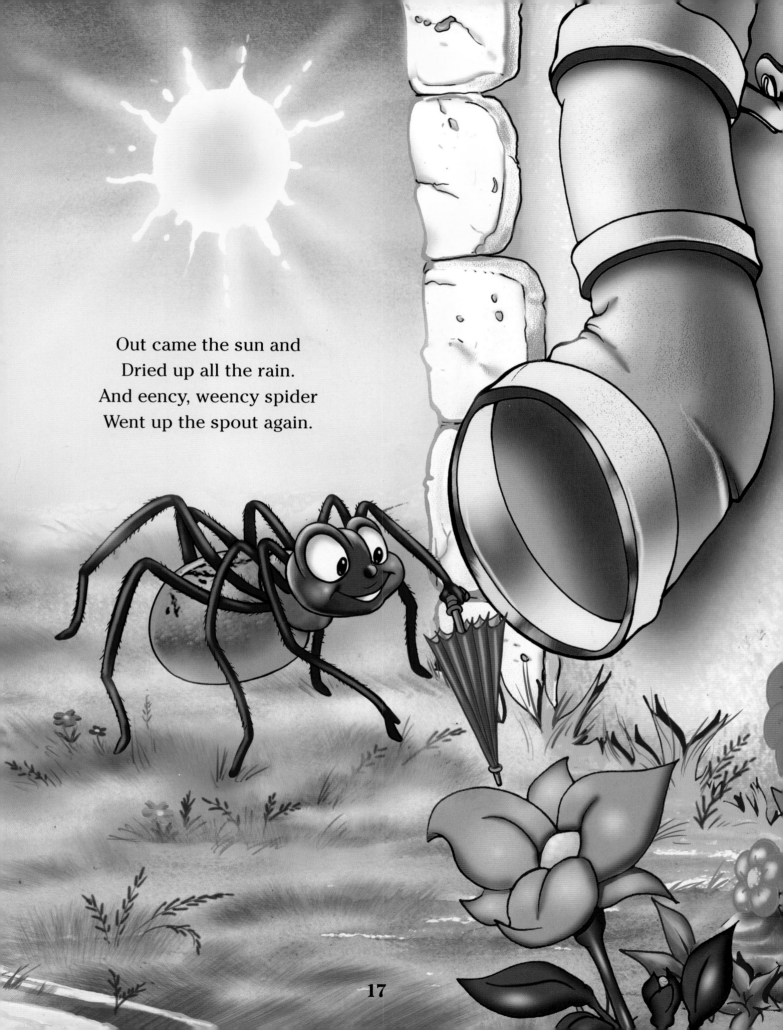

Out came the sun and
Dried up all the rain.
And eency, weency spider
Went up the spout again.

Mary Had a Little Lamb

Mary had a little lamb,
Its fleece was white as snow,
And everywhere that Mary went,
The lamb was sure to go.

18

It followed her to school one day,
That was against the rule,
It made the children laugh and play,
To see a lamb at school.

So the teacher turned it out,
But still it lingered near,
And waited patiently about,
Till Mary did appear.

"What makes the lamb love Mary so?"
The eager children cry.
"Why, Mary loves the lamb, you know,"
The teacher did reply.

21

One, Two, Buckle My Shoe

One, two,
Buckle my shoe;
Three, four,
Knock at the door;

Five, six,
Pick up sticks;
Seven, eight,
Lay them straight;

Nine, ten,
A good, fat hen;
Eleven, twelve,
Dig and delve;

24

Thirteen, fourteen,
Maids a-courting;
Fifteen, sixteen,
Maids in the kitchen;

Seventeen, eighteen,
Maids a-waiting;
Nineteen, twenty,
My plate's empty!

26

Red Sky at Morning

Red sky at morning,
Sailors take warning.
Red sky at night,
Sailor's delight.

Rock-a-Bye, Baby

Rock-a-bye, baby,
In the tree top.
When the wind blows,
The cradle will rock.

When the bough breaks,
The cradle will fall.
Then down will come baby,
Cradle and all.

Star Light, Star Bright

Star light, star bright,
The first star I see tonight.
I wish I may I wish I might,
Have the wish I wish tonight.

30

Wee Willie Winkie

Wee Willie Winkie runs through the town,
Upstairs and downstairs in his nightgown,
Rapping at the windows, crying through each lock,
"Are the children in their beds? It's now eight o'clock!"

Thirty Days Hath September

Thirty days hath September,
April, June, and November.
All the rest have thirty-one,
Save February, which alone,
Has twenty-eight—
Except in leap year, that's the time,
When February has twenty-nine.

Baa, Baa, Black Sheep

Baa, baa, black sheep,
Have you any wool?
Yes sir, yes sir,
Three bags full.

One for my master,
One for my dame,
And one for the little boy
Who lives down the lane.

Baa, baa, black sheep,
Have you any wool?
Yes sir, yes sir,
Three bags full.

Hickory,
Dickory, Dock!

Hickory, dickory, dock!
The mouse ran up the clock.
The clock struck one,
The mouse ran down.
Hickory, dickory, dock!

Eenie, Meenie, Minie, Moe

Eenie, Meenie, Minie, Moe,
Catch a tiger by the toe.
If he hollers, let him go,
Eenie, Meenie, Minie, Moe.

Hush, Little Baby

Hush, little baby, don't say a word,
Papa's going to buy you a mockingbird.

And if that mockingbird won't sing,
Papa's going to buy you a diamond ring.

And if that diamond ring turns brass,
Papa's going to buy you a looking glass.

And if that looking glass gets broke,
Papa's going to buy you a billy goat.

And if that billy goat won't pull,
Papa's going to buy you a cart and bull.

And if that cart and bull turn over,
Papa's going to buy you a dog named Rover.

And if that dog named Rover won't bark,
Papa's going to buy you a horse and cart.

And if that horse and cart fall down,
You'll still be the sweetest little baby in town.

I Love Little Kitty

I love little kitty,
Her coat is so warm,
And if I don't hurt her,
She'll do me no harm.

So I'll not pull her tail,
Nor drive her away,
But kitty and I,
Together will play.

43

It's Raining, It's Pouring

It's raining, it's pouring,
The old man is snoring.
He went to bed,
And bumped his head,
And couldn't get up in the morning.

Jack Be Nimble

Jack, be nimble,
Jack, be quick,
Jack, jump over the candlestick.

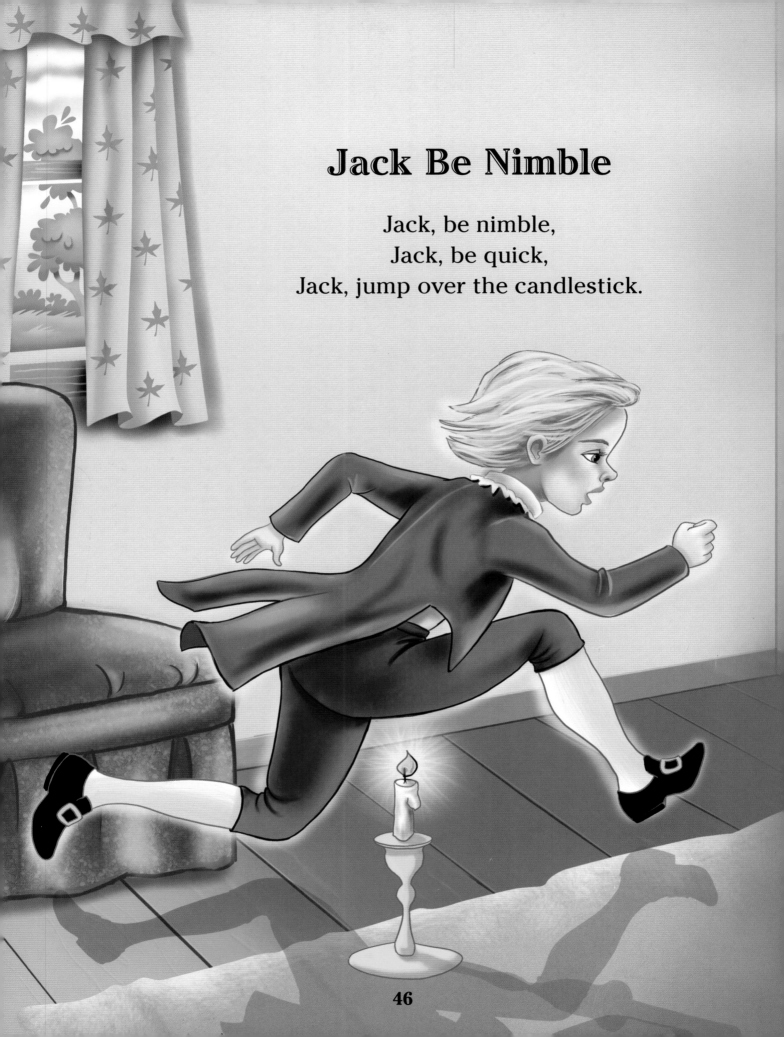

Little Boy Blue

Little Boy Blue,
Come blow your horn.
The sheep's in the meadow,
The cow's in the corn.

47

Where is the boy
Who looks after the sheep?
"He's under the haystack,
Fast asleep."

Will you wake him?
"No, not I,
For if I do,
He'll be sure to cry."

49

Little Miss Muffet

Little Miss Muffet,
Sat on a tuffet,
Eating her curds and whey.
There came a big spider,
Who sat down beside her,
And frightened Miss Muffet away.

Mary, Mary, Quite Contrary

Mary, Mary, quite contrary,
How does your garden grow?
With silver bells and cockle shells,
And pretty maids all in a row.

51

Peter, Peter, Pumpkin Eater

Peter, Peter, pumpkin eater,
Had a wife but couldn't keep her.
He put her in a pumpkin shell,
And there he kept her very well.

Peter, Peter, pumpkin eater,
Had another, but didn't love her.
Peter learned to read and spell,
And then he loved her very well.

The Queen of Hearts

The Queen of Hearts,
She made some tarts,
All on a summer's day.
The Knave of Hearts,
He stole the tarts,
And took them clean away.

The King of Hearts,
Called for the tarts,
And beat the Knave full sore.
The Knave of Hearts,
Brought back the tarts,
And vowed he'd steal no more.

Ring Around the Rosie

Ring around the rosie,
A pocket full of posies,
Ashes, ashes,
We all fall down.

The King has sent his daughter,
To fetch a pail of water,
Ashes, ashes,
We all fall down.

The birds upon the steeple,
Sit high above the people,
Ashes, ashes,
We all fall down.

The wedding bells are ringing,
The boys and girls are singing,
Ashes, ashes,
We all fall down.

Ladybug, Ladybug

Ladybug, ladybug, fly away home!
Your house is on fire, your children are gone.
All but one, and her name is Anne,
And she crept under the pudding pan.

Ladybug, ladybug, fly away home!
The field mouse is gone to her nest,
The daisies have shut up their sleepy red eyes,
And the bees and the birds are at rest.

Ladybug, ladybug, fly away home!
The glowworm is lighting her lamp,
The dew's falling fast, and your fine speckled wings
Will flag with the close-clinging damp.

Ladybug, ladybug, fly away home!
The fairy bells tinkle afar.
Make haste or they'll catch you and harness you fast
With a cobweb to Oberon's car.

Peter Piper

Peter Piper picked a peck of pickled peppers.
A peck of pickled peppers Peter Piper picked.

If Peter Piper picked a peck of pickled peppers,
Where's the peck of pickled peppers Peter Piper picked?

I Had a Little Nut Tree

I had a little nut tree, nothing would it bear,
But a silver nutmeg and a golden pear.
The King of Spain's daughter came to visit me,
And all was because of my little nut tree.
I skipped over water, I danced over the sea,
And all the birds in the air couldn't catch me.

Twinkle, Twinkle, Little Star

Twinkle, twinkle, little star,
How I wonder what you are.
Up above the world so high,
Like a diamond in the sky.
Twinkle, twinkle, little star,
How I wonder what you are.

When the blazing sun is gone,
When he nothing shines upon,
Then you show your little light,
Twinkle, twinkle, through the night.
Twinkle, twinkle, little star,
How I wonder what you are.

Then the traveler in the dark,
Thanks you for your tiny spark.
He could not see which way to go,
If you did not twinkle so.
Twinkle, twinkle, little star,
How I wonder what you are.

69

Higgledy, Piggledy

Higgledy, Piggledy, my black hen,
She lays eggs for gentlemen;
Sometimes nine, and sometimes ten.
Higgledy, Piggledy, my black hen!

Yankee Doodle

Yankee Doodle went to town,
Riding on a pony.
He stuck a feather in his hat
And called it macaroni.

Yankee Doodle, keep it up,
Yankee Doodle Dandy,
Mind the music and the step,
And with the girls be handy.

Father and I went down to camp,
Along with Captain Gooding,
And there we saw the men and boys,
As thick as hasty pudding.

There was Captain Washington,
Upon a slapping stallion,
Giving orders to his men,
I guess there were a million.

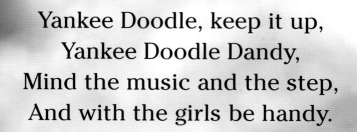

Yankee Doodle, keep it up,
Yankee Doodle Dandy,
Mind the music and the step,
And with the girls be handy.

Little Tom Tucker

Little Tom Tucker,
Sings for his supper.
What shall he eat?
White bread and butter.

How will he cut it,
Without any knife?
How will he marry,
Without any wife?

There Was a Crooked Man

There was a crooked man,
And he went a crooked mile.
He found a crooked sixpence,
Against a crooked stile.

He bought a crooked cat,
Which caught a crooked mouse,
And they all lived together,
In a crooked little house.

This Little Piggy

This little piggy went to market.
This little piggy stayed at home.
This little piggy had roast beef.
This little piggy had none.
This little piggy cried, "Wee, wee, wee!"
All the way home.

Three Blind Mice

Three blind mice, three blind mice,
See how they run, see how they run!
They all ran after the farmer's wife,
Who cut off their tails with a carving knife.
Did you ever see such a sight in your life,
As three blind mice?

Three Little Kittens

Three little kittens, they lost their mittens,
And they began to cry,
Oh, mother dear, we sadly fear,
That we have lost our mittens.

Lost your mittens! You naughty kittens!
Then you shall have no pie.
Meow, meow, meow, meow,
Then you shall have no pie.

The three little kittens, they found their mittens,
And they began to sing,
Oh, mother dear, see here, see here!
See, we have found our mittens.

84

You found your mittens! You good little kittens!
Then you shall have some pie.
Purr-r, purr-r, purr-r, purr-r,
Then you shall have some pie.

The three little kittens put on their mittens,
And soon ate up the pie.
Oh, mother dear, we greatly fear,
That we have soiled our mittens.

Soiled your mittens! You naughty kittens!
Then she began to sigh.
Meow, meow, meow, meow,
Then she began to sigh.

The three little kittens, they washed their mittens,
And hung them up to dry.
Oh, mother dear, look here, look here!
See, we have washed our mittens.

Washed your mittens! You clever kittens!
But I smell a rat close by.
Hush, hush, hush, hush,
I smell a rat close by.

Jack Sprat

Jack Sprat could eat no fat,
His wife could eat no lean.
And so, between them both, you see,
They licked the platter clean.

Jack ate all the lean,
Joan ate all the fat.
The bone they picked it clean,
Then gave it to the cat.

Little Jack Horner

Little Jack Horner,
Sat in the corner,
Eating a Christmas pie.

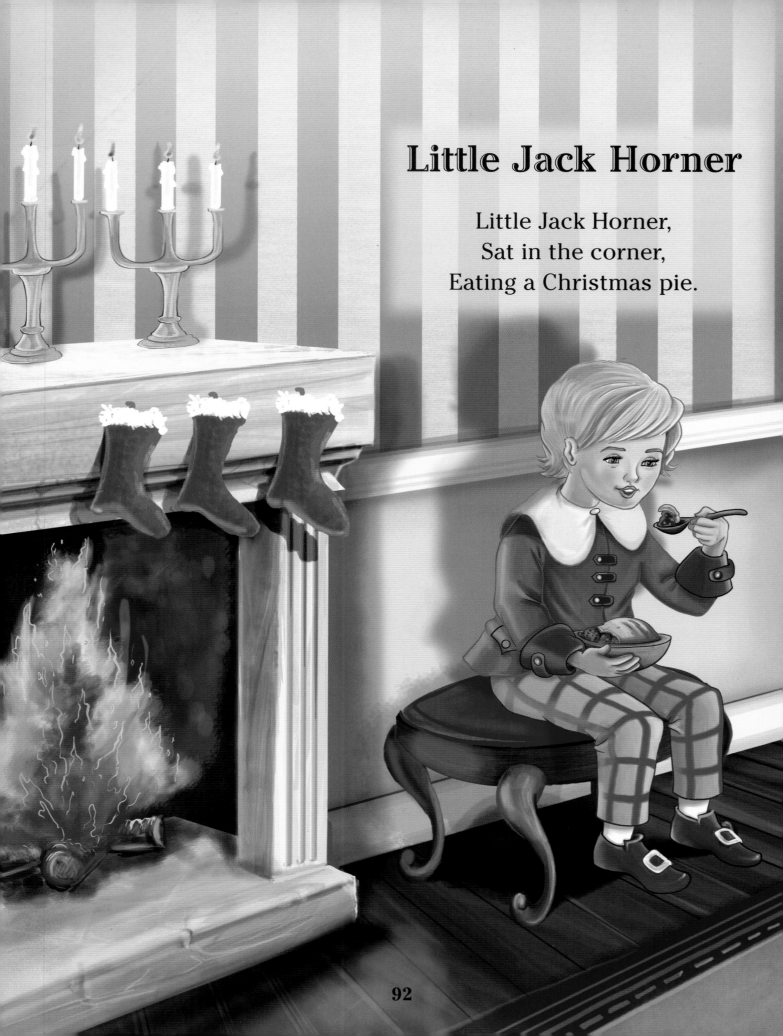

He stuck in his thumb,
And pulled out a plum,
And said, "What a good boy am I!"

Humpty Dumpty

Humpty Dumpty sat on a wall.
Humpty Dumpty had a great fall.
All the king's horses,
And all the king's men,
Couldn't put Humpty together again.

Rub-a-Dub-Dub

Rub-a-dub-dub,
Three men in a tub,
And how do you think they got there?
The butcher, the baker,
The candlestick maker—
They all jumped out of a rotten potato!
'Twas enough to make a fish stare.

I Saw a Ship A-Sailing

I saw a ship a-sailing,
A-sailing on the sea.
And, oh, it was all laden,
With pretty things for thee!

There were comfits in the cabin,
And apples in the hold.
The sails were made of silk,
And the masts were made of gold.

The four and twenty sailors,
That stood between the decks,
Were four and twenty mice,
With gold chains about their necks.

The captain was a duck,
With a packet on his back.
And when the ship began to move,
The captain said, "Quack! Quack!"

There Was a Little Girl

There was a little girl,
Who had a little curl,
Right in the middle of her forehead.
When she was good,
She was very, very good,
But when she was bad she was horrid.

Little Bo Peep

Little Bo Peep has lost her sheep,
And can't tell where to find them.
Leave them alone, and they'll come home,
Wagging their tails behind them.

Little Bo Peep fell fast asleep,
And dreamed she heard them bleating.
But when she awoke she found it a joke,
For they were still all fleeting.

Then up she took her little crook,
Determined for to find them.
She found them indeed, but it made her heart bleed,
For they'd left their tails behind them.

It happened one day, as Bo Peep did stray
Over a meadow hard by,
That there she espied their tails, side by side,
All hung on a tree to dry.

She heaved a sigh and wiped her eye,
Then over the hills she raced,
And tried what she could, as a shepherdess should,
So each tail would be properly placed.

There Was an Old Woman Who Lived In a Shoe

There was an old woman
Who lived in a shoe.
She had so many children
She didn't know what to do.
She gave them some broth,
Without any bread,
Then kissed them all quickly
And sent them to bed.

Old Mother Hubbard

Old Mother Hubbard,
Went to the cupboard,
To get her poor dog a bone,
But when she got there,
The cupboard was bare,
And so the poor dog had none.

She went to the baker's
To buy him some bread,
But when she came back
The poor dog was dead.

She went to the undertaker's
To buy him a coffin,
But when she came back
The poor dog was laughing.

She took a clean dish
To get him some tripe,
But when she came back
He was smoking a pipe.

She went to the fish shop
To buy him some fish,
And when she came back
He was licking the dish.

She went to the hatter's
To buy him a hat,
But when she came back
He was feeding the cat.

She went to the barber's
To buy him a wig,
But when she came back
He was dancing a jig.

113

She went to the grocer's
To buy him some fruit,
But when she came back
He was playing the flute.

She went to the tailor's
To buy him a coat,
But when she came back
He was riding a goat.

She went to the cobbler's
To buy him some shoes,
But when she came back
He was reading the news.

She went to the seamstress
To buy him some linen,
But when she came back
The dog was a-spinning.

She went to the hosier's
To buy him some hose,
But when she came back
He was dressed in his clothes.

The dame made a curtsy,
The dog made a bow.
The dame said, "Your servant,"
The dog said, "Bow wow!"

The Little Robin

The little robin grieves
When the snow is on the ground,
For the trees have no leaves,
And no berries can be found.

The air is cold, the worms are hid.
For robin here, what can be done?
Let's throw around some crumbs of bread,
And then he'll live till snow is gone.

Simple Simon

Simple Simon met a pieman
Going to the fair.
Simple Simon asked the pieman,
"Let me taste your ware."

Said the pieman to Simple Simon,
"Show me first your penny."
Simple Simon told the pieman,
"Indeed I have not any."

123

Simple Simon went out fishing
For to catch a whale.
All the water he had got
Was in his mother's pail!

Simple Simon went to see
If plums grew on a thistle.
He pricked his finger very much,
Which made poor Simon whistle.

He went to catch a dickey bird,
And thought he could not fail,
Because he'd found a little salt
To put upon its tail.

He went for water with a sieve,
But soon it all ran through.
And now poor Simple Simon
Bids you a fond adieu.

Sing a Song of Sixpence

Sing a song of sixpence,
A pocket full of rye,
Four and twenty blackbirds,
Baked in a pie.

When the pie was opened,
The birds began to sing.
Was not that a dainty dish
To set before the King?

The King was in the counting-house,
Counting out his money.
The Queen was in the parlor,
Eating bread and honey.

130

The Maid was in the garden,
Hanging out the clothes.
Down came a little blackbird
And snapped off her nose!

There Was an Old Woman
Tossed Up In a Basket

There was an old woman
Tossed up in a basket,
Seventeen times as high as the moon.
Where she was going,
I just had to ask it,
For in her hand she carried a broom.

"Old woman, old woman,
Old woman," said I,
"Please tell me, please tell me,
Why you're up so high?"
"I'm sweeping the cobwebs
Down from the sky,
And I will be with you
By and by."

The House That Jack Built

This is the house that Jack built.

This is the malt
That lay in the house that Jack built.

This is the rat,
That ate the malt,
That lay in the house that Jack built.

This is the cat,
That killed the rat,
That ate the malt,
That lay in the house that Jack built.

This is the dog,
That worried the cat,
That killed the rat,
That ate the malt,
That lay in the house that Jack built.

This is the cow with the crumpled horn,
That tossed the dog,
That worried the cat,
That killed the rat,
That ate the malt,
That lay in the house that Jack built.

This is the maiden all forlorn,
That milked the cow with the crumpled horn,
That tossed the dog,
That worried the cat,
That killed the rat,
That ate the malt,
That lay in the house that Jack built.

This is the man, all tattered and torn,
That kissed the maiden all forlorn,
That milked the cow with the crumpled horn,
That tossed the dog,
That worried the cat,
That killed the rat,
That ate the malt,
That lay in the house that Jack built.

This is the priest, all shaven and shorn,
That married the man, all tattered and torn,
That kissed the maiden all forlorn,
That milked the cow with the crumpled horn,
That tossed the dog,
That worried the cat,
That killed the rat,
That ate the malt,
That lay in the house that Jack built.

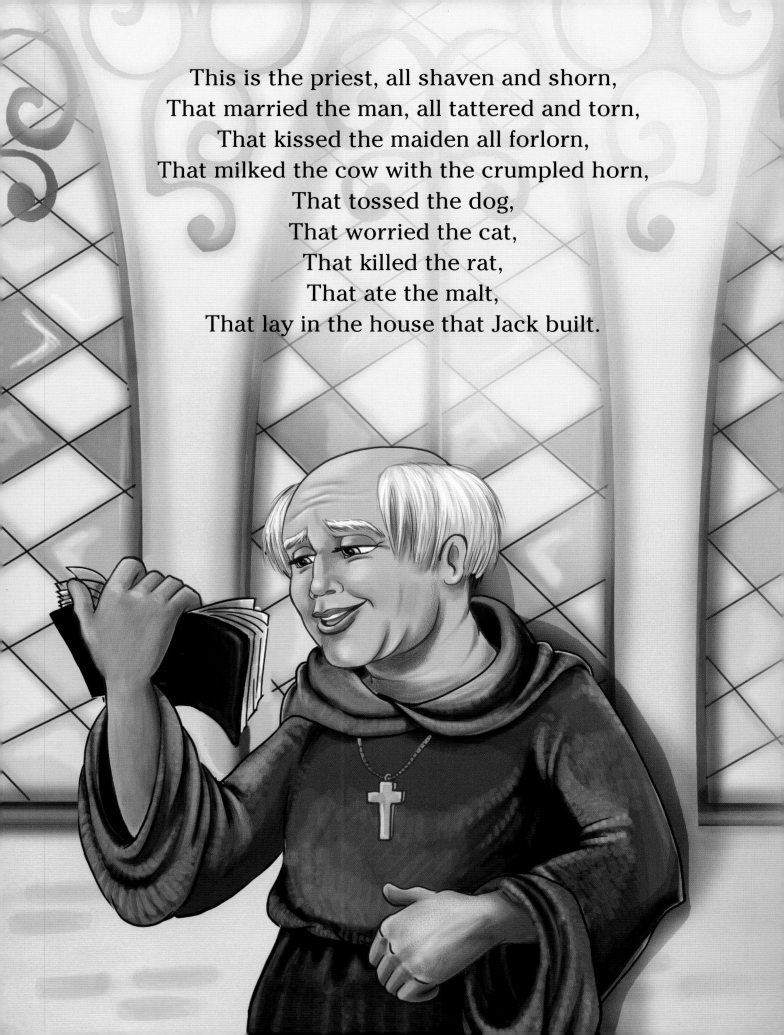

This is the cock that crowed in the morn,
That waked the priest, all shaven and shorn,
That married the man, all tattered and torn,
That kissed the maiden all forlorn,
That milked the cow with the crumpled horn,
That tossed the dog,
That worried the cat,
That killed the rat,
That ate the malt,
That lay in the house that Jack built.

This is the farmer who sowed the corn,
That kept the cock that crowed in the morn,
That waked the priest, all shaven and shorn,
That married the man, all tattered and torn,
That kissed the maiden all forlorn,
That milked the cow with the crumpled horn,
That tossed the dog,
That worried the cat,
That killed the rat,
That ate the malt,
That lay in the house that Jack built.

One, Two, Three, Four, Five

One, two, three, four, five,
Once I caught a fish alive.
Six, seven, eight, nine, ten,
But I let it go again.

Why did you let it go?
Because it bit my finger so.
Which finger did it bite?
The little one upon the right.

What Are Little Boys Made of?

What are little boys made of?
What are little boys made of?
Snips and snails, and puppy-dogs' tails;
That's what little boys are made of.

What are little girls made of?
What are little girls made of?
Sugar and spice, and all that's nice;
That's what little girls are made of.

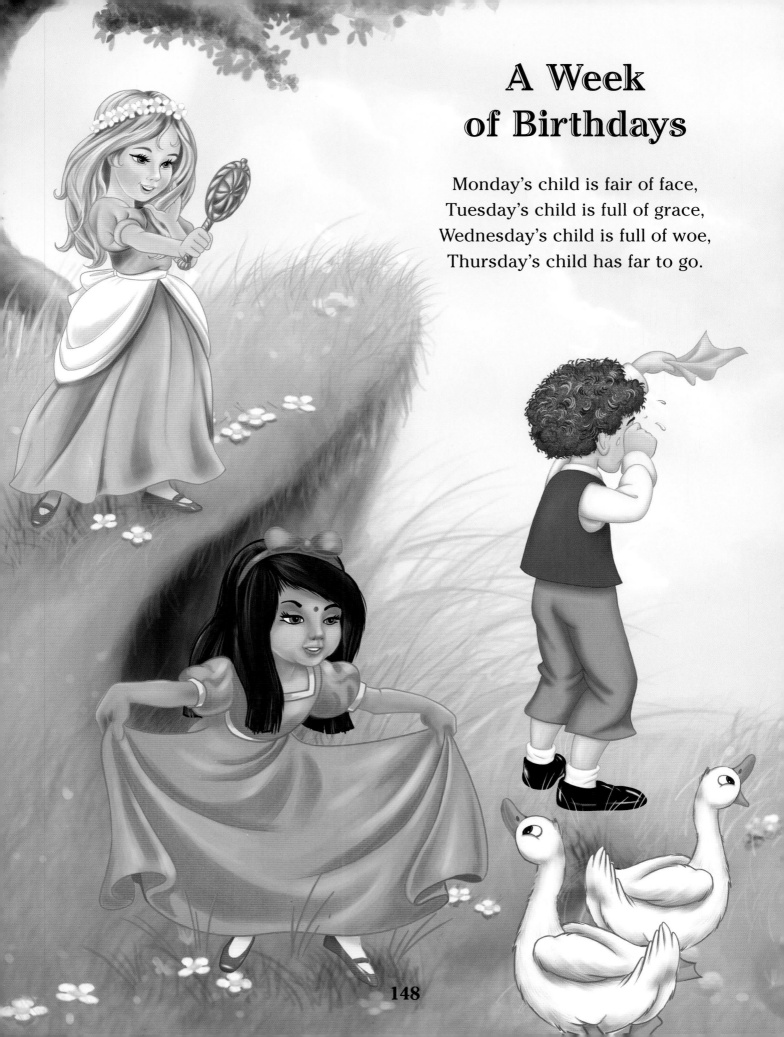

A Week of Birthdays

Monday's child is fair of face,
Tuesday's child is full of grace,
Wednesday's child is full of woe,
Thursday's child has far to go.

148

Friday's child is loving and giving,
Saturday's child works hard for a living,
But the child born on the Sabbath Day,
Is fair and wise and good and gay.

Ride a Cockhorse

Ride a cockhorse,
To Banbury Cross,
To see a fine lady
Upon a white horse,

150

Rings on her fingers,
And bells on her toes,
She shall have music
Wherever she goes.

Polly Put the Kettle On

Polly, put the kettle on,
Polly, put the kettle on,
Polly, put the kettle on,
We'll all have tea.

Sukey, take it off again,
Sukey, take it off again,
Sukey, take it off again,
They've all gone away.

Blow the fire and make the toast,
Put the muffins on to roast,
Blow the fire and make the toast,
We'll all have tea.

If I Had a Donkey

If I had a donkey that wouldn't go,
Would I beat him? Oh, no, no.
I'd put him in the barn and give him some corn,
The best little donkey that ever was born.

Oh, Dear! What Can the Matter Be?

Oh, dear! What can the matter be?
Dear, dear! What can the matter be?
Oh, dear! What can the matter be?
Johnny's so long at the fair.

156

He promised to buy me a trinket to please me,
And then for a smile, oh, he vowed he would tease me,
He promised to buy me a bunch of blue ribbons,
To tie up my bonnie brown hair.

Oh, dear! What can the matter be?
Dear, dear! What can the matter be?
Oh, dear! What can the matter be?
Johnny's so long at the fair.

He promised to bring me a basket of posies,
A garland of lilies, a gift of red roses,
A little straw hat to set off the blue ribbons,
That tie up my bonnie brown hair.

Oh, dear! What can the matter be?
Dear, dear! What can the matter be?
Oh, dear! What can the matter be?
Johnny's so long at the fair.

Curly-Locks

Curly-locks, curly-locks, wilt thou be mine?
Thou shalt not wash the dishes, nor yet feed the swine;
But sit on a cushion, and sew a fine seam,
And feed upon strawberries, sugar, and cream.

Pussy-Cat, Pussy-Cat

Pussy-cat, pussy-cat,
Where have you been?
I've been to London,
To visit the Queen.

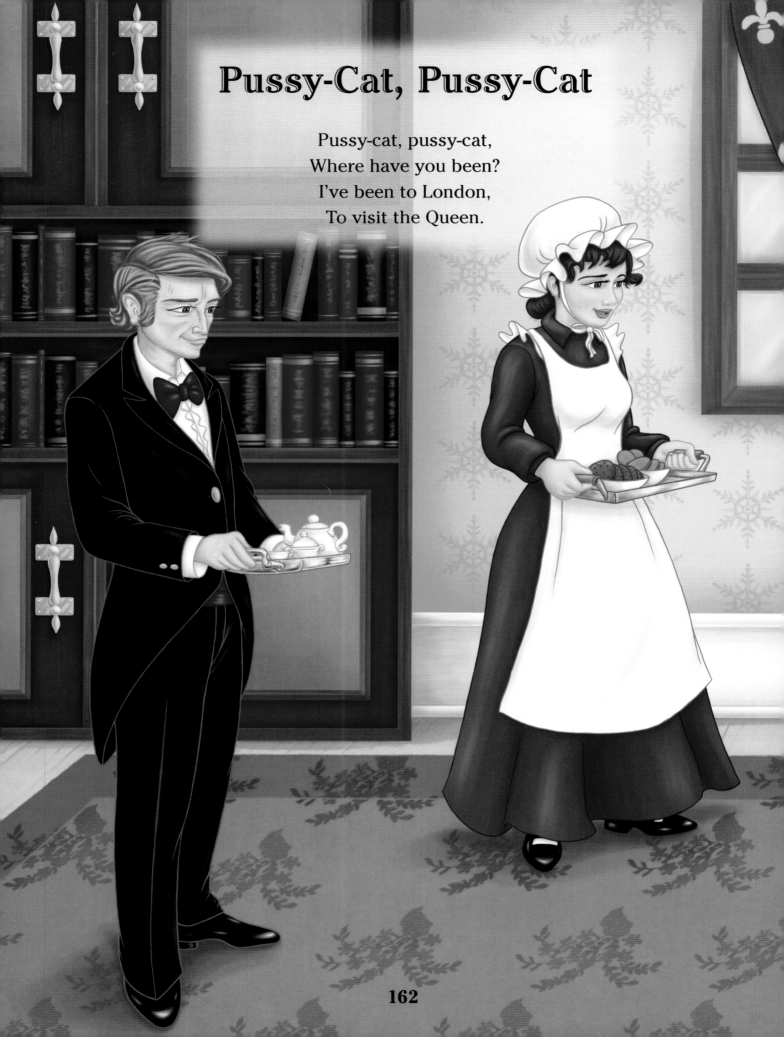

Pussy-cat, pussy-cat,
What did you there?
I frightened a little mouse
Under her chair.

Hot Cross Buns

Hot cross buns!
Hot cross buns!
One a penny, two a penny,
Hot cross buns!

If you have no daughters,
Give them to your sons;
One a penny, two a penny,
Hot cross buns.

A Tisket, A Tasket

A tisket, a tasket,
A green and yellow basket,
I wrote a letter to my love
And on the way I dropped it.

I dropped it, I dropped it,
And on the way I dropped it.
A little boy picked it up
And put it in his pocket.

Cock-a-Doodle-Do!

Cock-a-doodle-do!
My dame has lost her shoe,
My master's lost his fiddle-stick
And knows not what to do.

168

Cock-a-doodle-do!
What is my dame to do?
Till master finds his fiddle-stick,
She'll dance without her shoe.

Ding, Dong, Bell

Ding, dong, bell,
Kitty's in the well!
Who put her in?
Little Tommy Lin.
Who pulled her out?
Little Johnny Stout.

What a naughty boy was that
To try to drown poor kitty-cat.
Who never did him any harm,
But killed all the mice in his father's barn!

Here We Go 'Round the Mulberry Bush

Here we go 'round the mulberry bush,
The mulberry bush, the mulberry bush,
Here we go 'round the mulberry bush,
On a cold and frosty morning.

This is the way we wash our hands,
Wash our hands, wash our hands,
This is the way we wash our hands,
On a cold and frosty morning.

173

This is the way we wash our clothes,
Wash our clothes, wash our clothes,
This is the way we wash our clothes,
On a cold and frosty morning.

This is the way we go to school,
  Go to school, go to school,
This is the way we go to school,
  On a cold and frosty morning.

This is the way we come out of school,
Come out of school, come out of school,
This is the way we come out of school,
On a cold and frosty morning.

One For Sorrow

One for sorrow,
Two for joy,
Three for a girl,
Four for a boy,
Five for silver,
Six for gold,
Seven for secret,
Never to be told.

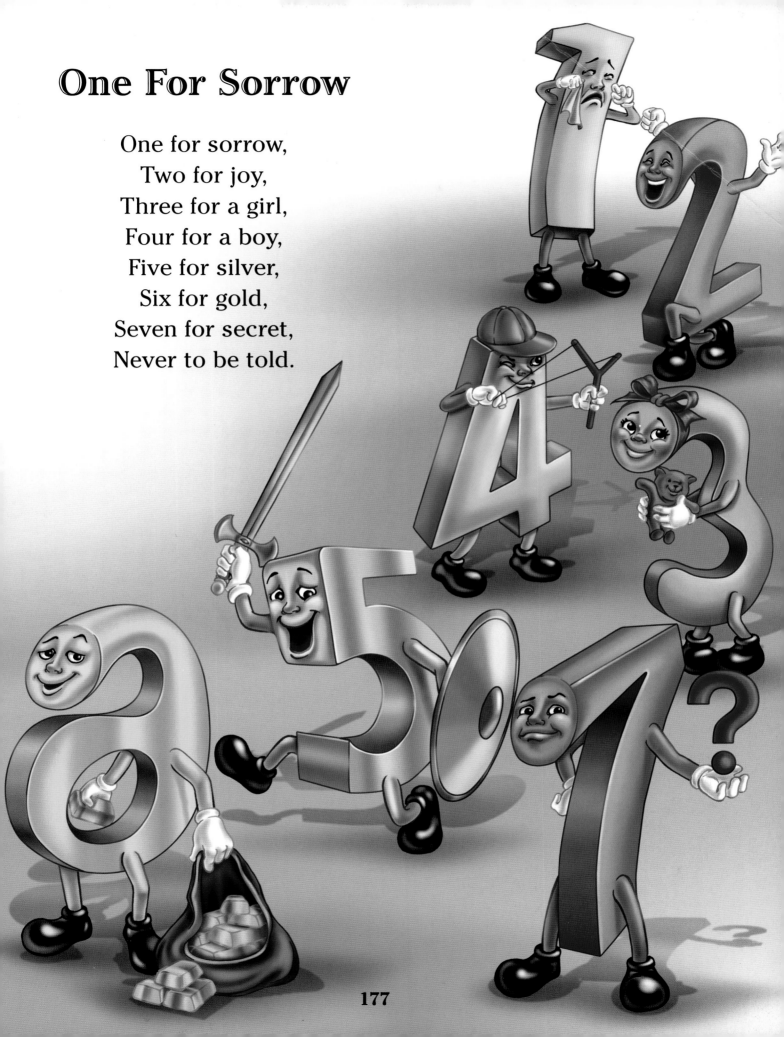

Three Young Rats

Three young rats
With black felt hats,

Three young ducks
With new straw flats,

Three young dogs
With curling tails,

Three young cats
With demi veils,

Went out to walk
With two young pigs,

In satin vests
And sorrel wigs;

But suddenly
It chanced to rain,

And so they all
Went home again.

If All the World

If all the world were apple pie,
And all the sea were ink,
And all the trees were bread and cheese,
What should we have for drink?

Lucy Locket

Lucy Locket lost her pocket,
Kitty Fisher found it;
Nothing in it, nothing in it,
But a ribbon round it.

183

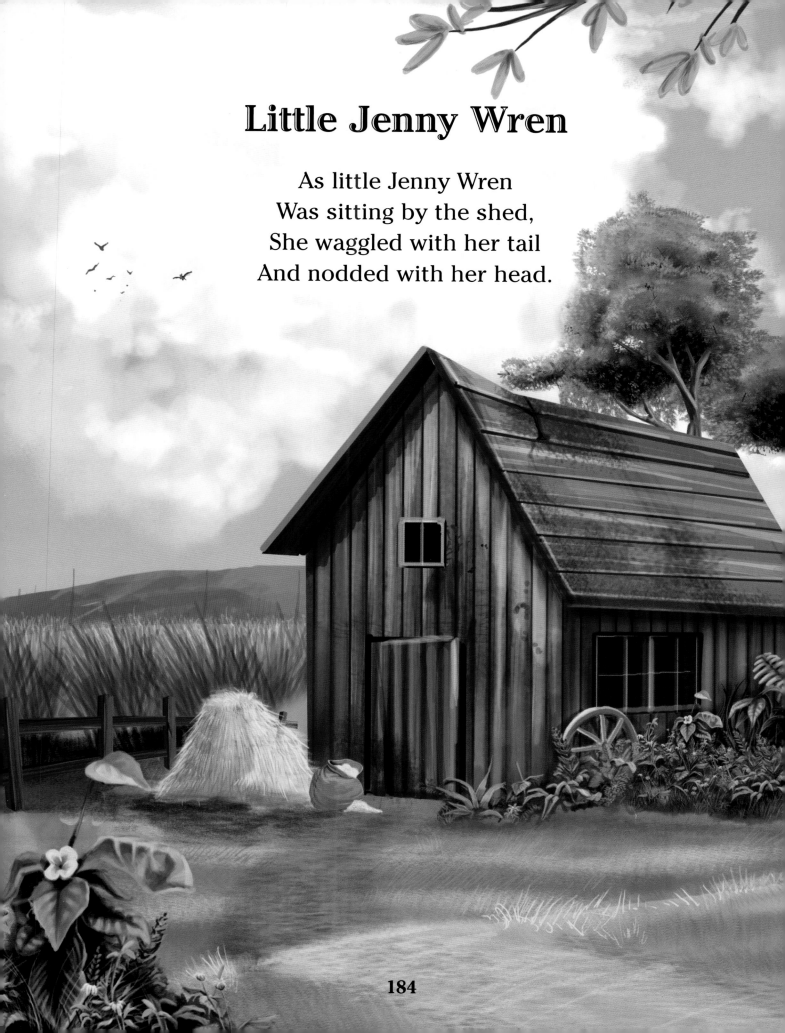

Little Jenny Wren

As little Jenny Wren
Was sitting by the shed,
She waggled with her tail
And nodded with her head.

184

She waggled with her tail
And nodded with her head,
As little Jenny Wren
Was sitting by the shed.

ABOUT THE RHYMES

Nursery rhymes have been recited to children and by children for hundreds of years. They are an integral part of most people's childhoods, but where did these rhymes originate from? Some nursery rhymes are more than just fun songs for adults and children to share with one another. In fact, the origins of many of the nursery rhymes in this treasury reflect events in history.

Their lyrics were often used as a way to mock royal and political events of the day in times when any direct challenge of the establishment could be punishable by death! It may seem strange that such events are still portrayed through children's nursery rhymes when many people today are unaware of the relationship between the two but, whether we realize their significance or not, nursery rhymes form a perpetual link between us and our past.

Because of the way spoken history is passed down, there are almost as many different interpretations of the rhymes' meanings as there are people who recite them, but the following are the most popular interpretations of some of the most well-known ones.

Jack and Jill

The roots of the story—or rhyme—
Jack and Jill allegedly lie in France.
It is said that the characters
represent King Louis XVI (Jack)
who was beheaded (or "broke his
crown") in 1793 during the French
Revolution when the monarchy
was abolished, followed later the
same year by his Queen Marie
Antoinette (Jill) who came "tumbling
after." The first publication date for the
lyrics of this rhyme is 1795, which ties in
with this event. *Jack and Jill* is also known
as *Jack and Gill*—variant spellings in nursery
rhymes are not uncommon, since they are usually
passed from generation to generation by word of mouth.

Rock-a-Bye, Baby

One interpretation of this rhyme is that it
reflects the observations of a young
pilgrim boy who had seen Native
Indian mothers suspend birch-bark
cradles from the branches of trees,
thus enabling the wind to rock their
children to sleep. Another is that it
dates back to eighteenth-century
England, and a family who lived in
a hollowed-out yew tree called the
"Betty Kenny Tree" in Shining Cliff
Woods, Derbyshire. The parents,
Kate and Luke Kennyon, had eight
children and are reputed to have
hollowed out a bough of the tree to
act as a cradle for their many offspring.

Star Light, Star Bright

This rhyme is believed to be of late-nineteenth century American origin, and the lyrics allude to the fantasy that you can wish upon a star. *Star Light, Star Bright* has no doubt been used on many occasions to quieten a child or children ready for bedtime as they look out of the window waiting to catch their very first glimpse of starlight that evening! A very popular rhyme, its first line has been used as the title for various books and songs in more recent times.

Baa, Baa, Black Sheep

The wool industry was vital to Britain's economy from the Middle Ages until the nineteenth century, so it's no surprise that such a long-established trade should be celebrated in a rhyme. Some say it has a historical connection to King Edward II (b. 1284–d. 1327). The best wool in Europe was produced in England, but the cloth workers from the cloth towns of Flanders—Bruges, Lille, Bergues, and Arras—were better at finishing trades like dying and "fulling" (cleansing, shrinking, and thickening the cloth), so the King encouraged them to improve the quality of the final English products.

Hickory, Dickory, Dock!

The first publication date for this rhyme is 1744. Investigation into the meanings of its words have lead people to believe that it has its roots in America. "Hickory" is a derived from the North American Indian word *pawcohiccora*—a kind of milk or oily liquor pressed from pounded hickory nuts from the pohickory tree. Dock is a species of plant that can used medicinally as an astringent and tonic—many of us will have experienced the soothing properties of the dock leaf after being stung by a nettle!

Jack Be Nimble

The most commonly agreed origin for this rhyme is the connection to Black Jack, an English pirate who was notorious for escaping from the authorities in the late sixteenth century. However, it could also be associated with the old tradition of "candle leaping" as practiced at some English fairs, which developed from an old sport of jumping over fires. In the lace-making schools of Wendover, Buckinghamshire, it was traditional to dance around the lace-makers' great candlestick, and it is thought this also led to the practice of jumping over the candlestick.

Mary, Mary, Quite Contrary

The Mary in this English rhyme is supposedly Mary Tudor, or Bloody Mary (b. 1498–d. 1533), who was the daughter of King Henry VIII of England. Queen Mary was a strict Catholic and the garden referred to is an allusion to graveyards which were increasing in size due to the killing of Protestants who dared to continue to adhere to the faith she was opposed to. The "silver bells and cockle shells" referred to were common words used to describe instruments of torture. "Maids" refers to a device called the Maiden which was used to behead people. This was the original guillotine!

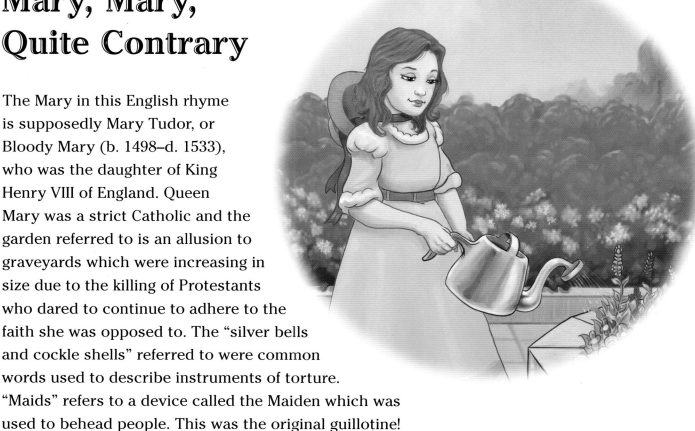

Ring Around the Rosie

This rhyme has its origin in English history during the Great Plague of London in 1665, or perhaps during the first outbreak in the 1300s. Plague symptoms included rosy, ring-shaped marks on the skin—"Ring around the rosie." Pockets and pouches were filled with sweet-smelling herbs, or "posies," that people carried in the belief that the disease was spread by bad smells. It is thought "Ashes, ashes" refers to the burning of the dead bodies. In the English version, *Ring-a-Ring-o' Rosie*, "Ashes, ashes" becomes "A-tishoo, a-tishoo," as sneezing was another plague symptom.

Yankee Doodle

The origins of this rhyme date back to fifteenth-century Holland and a harvesting song that began, "Yanker dudel doodle down." Later, the song poked fun at English Civil War leader Oliver Cromwell— "Yankee" was a mispronunciation of the Dutch word for "English" and "doodle" refers to a simpleton. But it was a British surgeon, Richard Schuckburgh, who wrote the words we know today, ridiculing the ragtag colonists fighting in the French and Indian War. Soon after, the British troops used the song to make fun of the American colonists during the American Revolutionary War (1775–1783), but the colonists adopted it as a rallying anthem of defiance and liberty.

Old Mother Hubbard

This rhyme alludes to King Henry VIII's (b. 1491–d. 1547) divorce from Queen Katherine of Aragon to enable him to marry his new love, Anne Boleyn. The most important churchman of the time, Cardinal Wolsey, displeased the King when he failed to ease this for him. Old Mother Hubbard represents Wolsey, the "doggie" King Henry, the "bone" the divorce, and the cupboard the Catholic Church. The divorce subsequently arranged by Thomas Cranmer resulted in the English church's break with Rome, the formation of the Church of England, and thus the demise of Old Mother Hubbard.

Ride a Cockhorse

This rhyme relates to Queen Elizabeth I of England's journey to Banbury, Oxfordshire, to visit a newly built stone cross. The lyrics "With rings on her fingers" relate to the jewelry she would have worn, and "bells on her toes" to the fashion of attaching bells to the pointed toes of shoes. This fashion actually originated from the Plantagenet era of English history that had ended over 70 years before the beginning of Elizabeth's reign, but it continued to be associated with the nobility for some time afterwards. When the Queen's carriage attempted the steep hill to Banbury Cross a wheel broke, so the Queen abandoned it in favor of a white cockhorse—a large stallion—to ride to the cross. The people of the town had provided minstrels to accompany her on her ascent—"she shall have music wherever she goes."